Tule Elk

Tule Elk

by Caroline Arnold / photographs by Richard R. Hewett
A Carolrhoda Nature Watch Book

 Carolrhoda Books, Inc./Minneapolis

LIBRARY OF CONGRESS CATALOGING-IN-PUBLICATION

Arnold, Caroline.
   Tule elk / by Caroline Arnold ; photographs by Richard R. Hewett.
     p.   cm.
   "A Carolrhoda nature watch book."
   Includes index.
   Summary: Describes the behavior and habitat of the tule elk.
   ISBN 0-87614-343-5 (lib. bdg.)
   1. Tule elk—Juvenile literature. [1. Tule elk. 2. Elk.]
I. Hewett, Richard, ill. II. Title.
QL737.U55A756   1989
599.73′57—dc19
                                       88-31565
                                         CIP
                                           AC

Manufactured in the United States of America

1 2 3 4 5 6 7 8 9 10 98 97 96 95 94 93 92 91 90 89

Thanks to Dr. Donald B. Siniff, Department of Ecology and Behavioral Biology, University of Minnesota, for his assistance with this book

We would like to express our appreciation to all the people who helped us on this project. Particular thanks go to Bill Barry, Eugene Hammock, and Tyler Conrad at the Tule Elk Reserve at Tupman, California; to Bill Cook at the State of California Department of Fish and Game, Sacramento, California; and to Dale McCullough, whose studies of the tule elk were an invaluable source of information.

This book is dedicated to the parents, students, and teachers in Taft, California, whose love of books and generous hospitality created the opportunity for us to discover the tule elk.

Additional photographs courtesy of: p. 17, Arthur Arnold; p. 43 (bottom), State of California, Department of Fish and Game

Grazing peacefully on grasses and shrubs, a herd of tule (TOO-lee) elk moves across the plain of California's Central Valley. In the mid-1800s, when pioneers descended the foothills surrounding the valley, they found thousands of elk just like these. In some places, there were so many animals that they darkened the plain as far as the eye could see. The California elk were similar to larger elk the pioneers had seen in the Rocky Mountains, and because they were often found in cattail swamps, or tule reeds, the settlers called them tule elk. Today, the valley is no longer a haven for wildlife. Instead of animals, there are ranches, roads, and towns spread across the plain. Where five hundred thousand tule elk once roamed, just a few hundred remain.

Until North America was discovered by Europeans, elk had few enemies. Although Native Americans hunted elk, they killed them only as they needed. They used elk meat for food; skins for clothing and shelter; teeth for decoration; and antlers for bows, spear tips, tools, and for hauling firewood. After Europeans came to this continent, however, the elk in the east slowly disappeared as the land was settled and forests were cut down. These people either killed the elk or drove them out of their natural grazing areas. In the west, however, elk continued to be abundant for several hundred years. But when gold was discovered in 1848, people poured into California's Central Valley and the foothills of the Sierra Nevada mountains that bordered the valley to the east. Those who did not prospect for gold began to settle in the valley to farm and ranch.

Elk provided meat and hides for the early pioneers. The elk were so plentiful that it seemed as if they would be available forever. However, as more elk were killed and more land was converted to agricultural use, the elk herds grew smaller. Finally, in 1873, the state of California recognized the need to protect these herds and passed a law that prohibited the shooting of elk. Unfortunately, the law came too late—the tule elk were almost **extinct**.

By the 1870s, much of the tule elk's former territory was being used for cattle ranches. The biggest of these was the ranch owned by the Miller and Lux Company near Buttonwillow, California. In 1875, several tule elk were discovered hiding in a swamp at the south end of the ranch. Henry Miller realized the importance of saving these animals and gave strict orders to everyone who worked for him to protect these elk.

Under Miller's protection, the females began to produce young elk, and although the herd grew slowly at first, its numbers climbed to over 400 by 1923. Most, if not all, of the tule elk alive today are the descendents of those animals.

As the elk herd on the Miller and Lux property grew, it began to cause considerable damage. Elk can create a lot of problems for ranchers because they destroy crops or eat plants that would otherwise feed cattle and horses.

Beginning in 1904, attempts were made to move the elk from the Miller and Lux property to areas not normally used for farming. Eventually, two new herds were established elsewhere in California. The herd near Cache Creek usually has about 80 elk, the other herd has about 400 elk and is in the Owens Valley.

With the elk that remained in the Central Valley, a breeding herd was established in 1934 near the small town of Tupman. The animals were placed inside a large enclosure on 953 acres of land that was formerly part of the Miller and Lux ranch. It is a place where the elk can live in safety and are supplied with plenty of food and water. Several ponds have been built on the land to give the elk drinking water and places to wallow or bathe. Cattails, or tule reeds, grow around the edges of the ponds and provide hiding places for young elk. Usually, there are about 40 tule elk in the Tupman herd. Throughout the year, visitors can observe the tule elk at close range, and wildlife managers can monitor the animals and make sure that they stay healthy.

Elk came to the North American continent about two million years ago, traveling from Europe and Asia over an ice and land bridge at the Bering Straits. The elk changed little over the centuries and are considered to be the same species as the majestic red deer of Europe to which they are closely related. In places such as New Zealand, where both European red deer and North American elk have been imported as game animals, the two groups interbreed.

Members of the deer family are found all over Europe, Asia, Northern Africa, and the Americas. In North America, elk are one of the largest members of this group, second only to moose, which are distinguished by their huge, thick antlers. Other members of the deer family in North America are whitetail deer, which are commonly seen in woodland areas; mule deer, which are seen only in the west; and three species of caribou, which are found in Canada and Alaska. There is often some confusion about what to call animals in this group because of name differences in various parts of the world. For instance, in Europe, the animal North Americans call a moose is called an elk, and the animal North Americans call an elk is called a deer. In North America, elk are sometimes called by their Native American name, wapiti, as well.

The **species** name for North American elk and European red deer is *Cervus elaphus*. In different parts of the world, as groups of elk have adapted to new

living conditions, they have changed somewhat. Each of these different groups forms a subspecies, or a group within the species. All subspecies are similar and can breed with each other. Tule elk, which are one of three subspecies of elk in North America, have the scientific name *Cervus elaphus nannodes*.

Tule elk are the smallest elk that live in North America and are sometimes called dwarf elk or valley elk. Fully grown tule elk bulls (males) can weigh up to 680 pounds (306 kg) and are about 4 feet (1.2 m) tall at the shoulder. Cows (females) are slightly shorter and can weigh up to 450 pounds (202.5 kg).

The largest American elk is the Roosevelt elk (*Cervus elaphus roosevelti*). A Roosevelt elk bull is about 5 feet (1.5 m) tall at the shoulder and can weigh up to 1,200 pounds (540 kg). Cows weigh up to 650 pounds (292.5 kg). Roosevelt elk live in coastal rainforests and can be found along the West Coast from northern California to British Columbia. Like all elk, the Roosevelt elk enjoy being in water and frequently go into ponds to cool themselves off during hot weather.

Roosevelt elk: males

The Rocky Mountain elk (*Cervus elaphus nelsoni*) are between the tule elk and Roosevelt elk in size. Bulls weigh between 600 and 1,000 pounds (270-450 kg) and cows between 500 and 550 pounds (225-247.5 kg). They usually live in mountains and are found throughout the Rockies and in parts of southern Canada. There are more Rocky Mountain and Roosevelt elk than tule elk, and most of them live on national park or national forest lands, where they are protected. Because they live in more remote areas, neither group has been as endangered as the tule elk.

Among the three subspecies of elk there are slight differences in appearance and behavior. The focus of this book is on the tule elk, although much of the information that follows applies to other elk as well. The tule elk are adapted to life on the open plains of California, where the climate, landscape, and food supply is different from that of forested areas, where other elk live. Winters are not harsh on the California plains, so tule elk generally have shorter coats than either the Roosevelt or Rocky Mountain elk. In the summer heat, the tule elk's light-colored coats reflect the hot sun. Tule elk also have smaller bodies and shorter antlers than other elk. One reason for this may be that food supplies in the valley are less abundant than in cooler, wetter climates. By the end of a long, dry summer, grass may be scarce and the tule elk's smaller body size requires less food.

All elk, both bulls and cows, have sleek reddish coats in summer, with light tan patches on their rumps. In winter, the hair grows long and becomes dull in coloring. Bulls are generally larger than cows and have a mane of dark hair around the neck. Perhaps the most impressive difference between male and female elk are the magnificent antlers on the males' heads. These huge **racks**, which look like forked tree branches, can measure 5 feet (1.5 m) or more from the head to the tip of the antler on a tule elk bull and more on larger elk. Unlike horns, which are permanent growths on animals such as sheep, cattle, and antelope, new antlers are grown and shed each year. In each successive year, the antlers grow larger and heavier.

The main part of each antler is called the **beam**. The base of the beam is attached to the skull. Each beam has up to six smaller points, or **tines**, branching off of it.

In medieval Europe, the antlers of red deer were a prized trophy for hunters, with the largest antlers being the most valuable. People developed a system for naming the tines, which is still used today for all elk. The first is called the brow tine; the second is the bez or bey tine; the third is the trez or trey tine; and the fourth, which in mature bulls is usually the largest, is the royal or dagger point. The fifth and sixth tines are smaller and are called the sur-royals. Although a typical full-grown antler has six points, sometimes there are more.

At the age of one year, a tule elk bull has only a pair of single spikes about 10 inches (25.4 cm) long. The second set of antlers is usually 25 to 30 inches (63.5-76.2 cm) long, with several small tines. In the bull's third year, the antlers are about the same length but heavier and stronger. Each year, the antlers grow back stronger, reaching their full size when the bull is six or seven years old. In a herd of young bulls, you can tell which animals are the oldest because they have the largest antlers.

For tule elk, antler growth usually begins in March or April, about a month after the previous set of antlers has been dropped off, or **cast**. The antlers are cast one at a time, and apparently the process is painless. The new antlers, which grow from small buds on the skull called **pedicels**, first appear as lumps on the head between the ears. By the end of April, they become short stumps. These quickly grow longer, reaching full length by July or August.

The new antlers are covered with a soft, tender skin called **velvet**. The velvet is filled with blood vessels that bring nutrients to the rapidly developing antlers. By the end of the summer, the antlers have finished growing. The velvet is no longer needed and falls off. During the week or so when the velvet is being shed, the elk rub their antlers against trees, fenceposts, or along the ground to help remove the velvet. When all the velvet is gone, the newly revealed antlers are a bright white and in their full glory.

In the spring, the male and female elk separate into two herds. Then, during July and August, the male elk rejoin the herd of females and young elk. By the end of August, the elk are ready for the mating season, which is called the **rut**. The rut usually lasts from late August to early October.

Elk cows usually begin to breed at the age of two, although they may be able to breed at one year. Bulls are able to breed at one year but usually do not get a chance until they are older and stronger. In the rutting season, bulls compete fiercely with each other for the privilege of mating with the females. Only the biggest and strongest bulls will mate.

Fights between bulls are common in the period just before and during the rutting season. A bull first announces his challenge to another bull by **bugling**. To bugle, he extends his neck, opens his mouth, and makes a whistling roar that is so loud it can be heard nearly one mile (1.6 km) away.

A fight between two bulls progresses through several stages, beginning with threats and ending with physical contact. At first, the two animals approach each other and face off. They will then stare at each other for several minutes. Sometimes, the weaker animal will back off when outstared by a stronger bull. If the fight continues, the two elk will approach each other, lower their heads, and swing their antlers along the ground, a behavior called **thrashing**.

At any point, one of the males may choose to retreat, but if the fight continues to an all-out battle, the two elk lunge at each other and lock antlers. Then, they push and shove and try to throw one another off balance. The loser is the one that is eventually forced to retreat.

Over a period of several weeks, the strongest bull drives all the others out of the herd. He becomes the **master elk** and takes charge of his **harem**, the female herd. He guards his harem closely and keeps the animals in a tight group. As each female becomes ready to breed, she mates with the master elk.

Meanwhile, the rejected bulls stay close. One by one they continue to challenge the master elk. Usually, the master elk is replaced several times during the rutting season. While he is master, each bull mates with the cows that are ready to breed. Only strong bulls can maintain a harem and have the chance to mate.

When the rut ends, fighting stops, and the males that had been driven out of the herd rejoin the females and the master elk. The elk stay together through the winter, moving about, grazing, and resting as a group. A typical herd has about 40 to 60 animals, although several herds may occupy the same general area, forming one large herd.

By November, the elk's heavier winter coats have finished growing. Although it seldom snows in the Central Valley, where tule elk live, nighttime winter temperatures often fall below freezing, and the elk need to have warm coats. Elk that live in the mountains usually migrate to warmer valleys in winter.

In spring, the bulls and cows separate into two herds. At this time of year, their long winter hairs are shed, revealing a sleek new coat underneath.

Baby elk are born about 8½ months after the mating season. By the end of April and the beginning of May, the female tule elk are ready to give birth. One by one, each pregnant female goes off into the tule reeds to find a protected spot where she can be alone. There, she gives birth to a single baby, which is called a calf. Twins are rarely born.

A newborn tule elk calf weighs between 18 and 30 pounds (8-13.5 kg). Its brown coat is speckled with white spots, which help it blend into its surroundings. Although it is able to stand on wobbly legs within minutes of its birth, it does not stay on its feet long.

During the first few weeks of life, in the safety of darkness, the tule elk calf may follow its mother as she feeds. But in the daytime, the calf stays hidden while its mother eats. If disturbed, the calf instinctively lowers its head against the ground and lies completely still. If a cow sees any animal approaching her calf, she chases it away. The main enemies of newborn calves are coyotes, bobcats, and mountain lions.

As is true of all **mammals**, the baby elk's first food is its mother's milk. The calf nurses from one of the four **teats** on its mother's underside. Each day, the calf grows bigger and stronger, gaining about one pound (.45 kg) a day. At the age of three weeks, the young calf is able to join the herd with its mother.

At first, the new calves stick close by their mothers' sides. As they grow older and more confident, they wander away to explore on their own.

Although milk is the main food during the first few months of life, an elk calf begins to nibble on tender shoots of grass as early as a few days after birth. As it grows older, grass and other plants become a larger part of its diet. By the age of five months, a calf no longer needs milk and is able to eat the same foods as adult elk.

By late July or early August, most of the calves have shed their spotted coats. The new coat is gray but will later turn brown like those of the adults. The calves will reach adult size when they are one year old. A calf can take care of itself by fall, but usually stays with its mother through the winter.

Like deer, moose, reindeer, and other members of the deer family, elk are herbivores. They eat grass, shrubs, and other plants. Like many animals in the deer family, elk are **ruminants**, which means that they are cud chewers. Food is chewed and swallowed. Then it is **regurgitated**, or coughed up, and swallowed again. This allows the food to be digested more thoroughly.

Elk have 24 teeth. Sharp teeth in the front of the mouth are used to snip off grass. Large flat teeth in the back of the mouth chew and grind food.

Most of the time, the tule elk can find enough grass and leaves to eat at the Tule Elk Reserve near Tupman, California. In periods when there has been little rain and food is scarce, however, rangers feed the elk nutritional pellets.

Tule elk are active both during the day and night, and they alternate periods of eating with periods of resting. Usually, they eat for about two hours then rest for about two hours. When resting, they lie down in open areas, where any possible danger can easily be seen or heard before it gets too close.

Because they are so large, elk in the wild have few natural enemies. For tule elk, mountain lions are possible predators, but like the elk, their population has been greatly reduced by people, so they don't pose much of a threat.

An elk has an excellent sense of smell and sense of hearing. If one member of a tule elk herd detects a strange smell or sound, it raises its head and flattens its ears. This posture warns the other elk that danger may be near and to be alert. The elk may also emit a barking noise in the direction of the possible intruder. Every elk in the herd will stop what it is doing and stare at the disturbance, and if it is identified as a danger, then all the elk will flee.

Elk prefer to run away from an enemy rather than to fight. At top speed, an elk can run 30 miles per hour (48 kph) for short distances. A herd of elk can maintain a steady running speed of 22 to 24 miles per hour (35.2-38.4 kph).

Once a year, usually in late summer, wildlife managers count the tule elk. In some cases, ear tags help identify individual animals. When there are too many elk in one area, some may starve because there is not enough food. Some people feel that the best way to keep the elk herd from growing too large is to allow people to hunt elk. Others object to hunting and feel that it would be better to move some of the elk to other locations. In a recent moving operation, a number of elk in the Owens Valley were captured and carried by helicopter to another area nearby. The new herd quickly adapted to the surroundings and began to multiply. This type of operation is difficult, however, because elk are hard to catch and because there are few places available that would make suitable new homes for elk.

Wild elk usually live for about 10 years, although in captivity they have been known to live for as long as 25 years. With care and protection, the tule elk have progressed from a subspecies that was almost extinct one hundred years ago, to one that has been reestablished in its natural home.

The near disappearance of the tule elk in California is an example of what happens when there is conflict between people and animals for space and natural resources. Wildlife managers today need to find ways in which animals like tule elk can coexist with people and live a healthy life in the wild. Tule elk are part of our natural heritage, which we need to preserve. Once it was feared that tule elk had become extinct. Luckily, through the work of many dedicated people, the elk were saved, and today, in several places in California, you can see tule elk and admire their majestic beauty.

GLOSSARY

beam: main stem of an elk's antler, the base of which is attached to the elk's skull

bugle: the mating call of a male elk, which sounds like a whistling roar

cast: the dropping off of antlers

extinct: when all the members of a species die

harem: the herd of female elk that forms during the mating season

mammals: animals that nourish their young with milk from their bodies

master elk: a strong male elk that takes charge of a female herd during the mating season

pedicels: the small buds on a male elk's skull from which new antlers grow

rack: a pair of antlers

regurgitate: to cough up from the stomach

ruminant: an animal that regurgitates food and has a four-chambered, complex stomach in which bacteria break down food for processing

rut: the elk's mating season, which usually lasts from late August to early September

species: a group of animals or plants that share similar characteristics

teat: the tip of a female mammal's udder or breast from which milk is drawn

thrash: type of challenge between male elk during the mating season. The elk lower their heads and swing their antlers along the ground.

tine: the part of an antler that branches off of the beam

velvet: the soft skin that surrounds and nourishes the developing antlers

INDEX

ABOUT THE AUTHOR

Caroline Arnold is the author of numerous widely acclaimed books for young readers, including the Carolrhoda Nature Watch titles *Saving the Peregrine Falcon* and *A Walk on the Great Barrier Reef*. Ms. Arnold is also an instructor in the UCLA extension writers' program. She lives in Los Angeles with her husband and their two children.

ABOUT THE PHOTOGRAPHER

Richard R. Hewett graduated from the Art Center School of Design, in California, with a major in photojournalism. He has illustrated more than 30 children's books and collaborated with Caroline Arnold on the Carolrhoda Nature Watch title *Saving the Peregrine Falcon*. He lives in Los Angeles with his wife.